D1396583

Living with a Single Parent

Living with a Single Parent

by MAXINE B. ROSENBERG

Bradbury Press / New York

Maxwell Macmillan Canada / Toronto
Maxwell Macmillan International
New York / Oxford / Singapore / Sydney

Bradbury Press
Macmillan Publishing Company
866 Third Avenue
New York, NY 10022

Maxwell Macmillan Canada, Inc.
1200 Eglinton Avenue East
Suite 200
Don Mills, Ontario M3C 3N1

Macmillan Publishing Company is part of the Maxwell Communication Group of Companies.

First Edition
Printed and bound in the United States of America
10 9 8 7 6 5 4 3 2 1

The text in this book is set in Baskerville.

LIBRARY OF CONGRESS CATALOGING-IN-PUBLICATION DATA

Rosenberg, Maxine B.
  Living with a single parent / by Maxine B. Rosenberg. — 1st ed.
    p.   cm.
  Includes bibliographical references (p.   ).
  Summary: Seventeen children from single-parent families describe how they cope with their circumstances.
  ISBN 0-02-777915-7
  1. Children of single parents—United States—Juvenile literature.
2. Single-parent family—United States—Juvenile literature.
[1. Single-parent family.] I. Title.
HQ777.4.R67   1992
306.85′6—dc20   92-3883

Acknowledgments

My grateful thanks to the following people and organizations who helped make this book possible: Eileen Holiber, Director of Big Brothers/Big Sisters program of the Family Services of Westchester, New York, for her time and interest; Jane Mattes, Director of Single Mothers by Choice; Andrea Troy of New York Singles Adopting Children, Inc.; James J. Campbell, Executive Director of Leake and Watts Children's Home; Lesbian Line of Westchester, for their efforts in helping me find the right people for this book; Marilyn Tribble and Jim Buhs, for trusting me to interview their friends; and most of all, the parents and the children who are a part of this book, for sharing their deepest feelings with me so others in similar situations might benefit from these experiences.

To Aunt Judy and Uncle Mike—
For letting me be their third child

Contents

Introduction

Today, in the United States, single parent families are no longer a rarity. Fifty percent of marriages end in divorce and twenty-six percent of babies are born to single women. There are other causes of single parent homes too, such as death of a parent and single parent adoptions.

While most families (79 percent) are still headed by two parents (this includes remarriages), in 1989, the Census Bureau indicated that 17 percent have just a mother at home and 4 percent, only a father. Indeed, the single parent household is becoming a common family group, with no ethnic or sociologic boundaries.

Because most single parent families are formed

1

through separation and divorce, most of the stories in this book are told by the children of those families. Also included, though, are bereaved children and children living with an unwed mother, as well as a child adopted by a single parent and a child whose unmarried mother chose to have a baby through artificial insemination. Stories of girls living with just a dad, or boys living with just a mom, children who have grown up in extreme poverty, children whose absentee parent lives thousands of miles away, children living with a gay parent, only children, and children with siblings are also represented.

While I realize that many children living with a single parent have continued difficulty adjusting to their family situation, I purposely have not selected those stories for the book. Instead, I have chosen recountings of children who are finding ways to cope, so that others in similar circumstances may learn from their strategies.

To find subjects for this book, I contacted support groups, family service agencies, school nurses, and guidance counselors, asking each to recommend children who are both verbal and insightful and who might benefit from sharing their feelings and experiences. (Naturally, the parents' permission was necessary.) I said that if there was a sibling who could strengthen a brother's or sister's story, I would include that child in the chapter, but I did not want to have more than two combined-sibling chapters in the whole book.

After a family agreed to be part of the project, I called

to set up a date to meet the child. Oddly, one parent after another insisted I interview all their children regardless of whether they had all been referred to me or not. During my many years of writing books on children's topics, this had never happened to me before. Even more interesting was the fact that the children themselves were pushing to be in the book. While I agreed to go along with the families' wishes, I told them that I couldn't promise all the siblings' stories would appear in print.

Only after interviewing the siblings did I realize why these brothers and sisters were adamant about talking to me. Because so many mothers and fathers in single parent homes work full-time, siblings rely on one another for protection and decision-making while the parent is away. They feel very connected and consider themselves a unit. Once I realized this, I decided to include all of their stories.

What particularly impressed me after interviewing the children for this book was their keen sensitivity and appreciation of their parent's situation. While not minimizing their own problems, the children were well aware of their parent's burdens, and in big and small ways, they tried to lighten the load.

At one time or another most of the children in this book have had counseling either privately or through a school or agency. All agreed that talking to a counselor helped them to understand things better.

Yet despite this, many still were embarrassed by their

family situation and tried to hide it from their peers. Being surrounded by others who also lived with single parents made little difference to them. In their minds, they stood out for being in one parent families. To them, a "normal" family meant both a mother and father at home.

Most interviews lasted one to two hours. And more time was spent with the children as I photographed them. Usually I had further questions after I'd transcribed the tapes, so I'd call and speak to the children and/or their parents again. One twelve-year-old girl said, "Talking to you has helped me. I could go on and on. Is there any more you want to ask me?"

A parent of two siblings said, "Your behind-the-scenes interviewing has helped my family so much. It's opened up new areas we've never talked about and has brought us closer together."

All the families agreed to retain their real names and to be photographed by me.

In this book, my main goal is to help children learn ways to deal with issues they are facing in single parent homes. Above all, I want them to see that they are not alone in their problems and that it's often comforting to share their feelings with others.

Without the cooperation of the children who volunteered to tell their stories, I could never have accomplished this task. My grateful thanks go to all of them and to their families.

"I thought it was up to me to make things run smoothly."

Logan,
age 13

Just before I was seven, something happened in my family that I will never forget. Dad had eaten watermelon in the room he and Mom used to share and he left the plate with the rind there. When Mom saw it, she was furious and the next thing I knew, my parents were having a big fight. Right after, Dad left.

Although my parents' arguing was nothing new, I didn't think their marriage would ever break up. When Dad walked out, I was sure he would come back. My brother, Sloan, who was five, and my sister, Dane, who was just four, thought he was coming back, too. Not until I visited him in his own apartment did I understand what was going on. Then I cried and cried.

At first Dad paid child support but then stopped. This made Mom angry because Dad was a lawyer and made good money. And it confused me. He wouldn't help pay the bills, yet he was nice enough to buy us a dog so we'd have something special to look forward to at his house. There was so much I didn't understand.

With little money coming in, Mom had to work two jobs. She helped students who had educational problems and she taught at a college. During the week, we rarely saw her. Instead, Grandma, who used to visit now and then, started coming every day to take care of us. She made dinner if Mom had to work late and also tidied up the inside and outside of the house. If I needed something, I asked Grandma for it, not my mother, because Grandma was the one who was paying for our food and clothing. This made me feel peculiar. I wanted one of my parents to be in charge.

At school too, I felt different, since my parents were among the first to break up. In class, I'd drift off, thinking about my home situation. Soon it affected my work. Although I was only in first grade, I started having serious reading and spelling problems. Those subjects still give me a hard time, but not as bad as back then.

It was difficult for me to adjust to living with a single parent. While other dads were coming home to their families at night, mine was somewhere else. He wasn't around to help me with my homework or play a game of catch with me on weekends.

Mom tried to keep up the things we had done when

Dad lived here, like playing Wiffle ball and going camping and white water rafting, but she wasn't a dad. I needed my father, yet I didn't want him living with us if I'd have to hear the arguing again.

When Mom saw how unhappy I was and how sad my brother and sister were too, she arranged for us to go to family counseling once a week. She went too, and it helped some. But I was still having problems. So the following year, Mom spoke to the school psychologist, who agreed to see me twice a week.

It took me a while to open up in counseling. In the beginning I'd answer the questions the psychologist asked about my home life, but I wouldn't say a word after that. Then, little by little, I started bringing up subjects on my own. One thing that really bothered me was the amount of responsibility I had taken on since Mom became a single parent. By now, Grandma was living half the year in Florida, and although we had sitters, none was terrific, so I felt I had better keep an eye on things.

Whenever we three kids came in from school to an empty house, I thought it was up to me to make things run smoothly. I'd go over the list of chores Mom had left for us, and I'd think I had to make sure everything got done before she came home.

If the list said, "Sloan's day to do laundry," I'd tell my brother to get busy. Instead, he'd sit there and do nothing. So I'd bug him, and then we'd have a fight. What really bothered me was that I had more jobs to do than Sloan and Dane. Their chores could be done in a few minutes. Then they'd be outside playing, while I'd still be indoors folding clothes.

The weirdest part was that Mom wasn't that fussy about the house until she became a single parent. But once Grandma started keeping things orderly, Mom got that way too, and this meant more work for me. Every time I'd compare my chores with the chores done by friends who lived with two parents, my list came out much longer.

Today Mom earns enough money, so Grandma doesn't have to support us as much. That makes me feel better. I'm glad Mom can do it on her own, even though her salary will always leave us a little deprived. We can't afford a large-screen TV like my friends have, or a new car. The only way we were able to replace our ratty couch was when our friends refurnished their living room and gave us their old couch.

I'm not thrilled about having so little money, yet it's taught me to watch what I spend. Instead of getting rid of my allowance in one shot the way many kids do, I save up for something special. With my allowance and what I earn from baby-sitting, I'm planning to buy a full-sized bed for my room so I won't have to sleep in a double-decker anymore. If Dad were here, he'd pay for the bed, and I could get myself something else. But I'd rather not have him and Mom under the same roof if it means hearing them fight.

Because we kids don't have a male figure around the house, Mom's gone out of her way to hire guys for baby-sitters. Steve stayed with us for one year, and now we have John, who's twenty-four and sleeps in. During the day he has a job, but he helps around the house for free room and board. He's fun to wrestle with and takes us fishing.

Also, Sloan and I each have a Big Brother. My Big Brother is Jean Luc. He's French, speaks three languages, and is good in engineering. The other day he brought home an old tractor lawn mower that someone had thrown out. The two of us took it apart and are now cleaning it up and putting in new gears.

I like him and John, my sitter, too. Yet Mom's the one I go to when something's troubling me. There's nothing I wouldn't tell her. The only problem is that she works such long hours that she's not always there when I need her. I wish she had more time to be with me alone so we could take quiet walks along the reservoir or work together in the yard. We don't even have to talk to each other. Being next to Mom is enough for me.

About a year ago Dad moved to Florida, and since then we kids only see him on holidays and for a few weeks during the summer. Whenever we visit, he tries to make up for lost time by taking us to so many places, which is tiring but fun. Having him so far away is another hard thing to get used to.

Because of my parents' divorce, I've been through a lot, but in some ways, it's helped me. I've learned to appreciate what Mom does for us, and I've become more caring about people. Recently my friend's mother died, and I told him how sorry I was to hear that. Other kids in school stayed clear of him because they were too scared.

As the years pass, I'm beginning to believe that my life isn't as bad as I once thought. When Dad left, I felt we got the short end of the stick because he didn't give us money. But now that Mom's in a group for divorced mothers, she tells me about families who are in worse shape. One father won't support his kids even though their mother doesn't work. Compared to them, I feel lucky.

Mom has held our family together, and even when things were hard, she didn't give up. Although I thought I was the one who was having it the worst, I realize today that Mom has had a difficult time, too. I used to wish that she and Dad would marry each other again, but I don't think that anymore. We're better off the way things are now.

"Since Mom's become a single parent, I don't get to see much of her."

Sloan,
age 11

Although I was only five the day Mom and Dad separated, I still remember that day. First they had a big fight. Then Dad packed his clothes, put them in the car, and went away. Logan, my older brother, and I thought Dad was going on a trip. Dane, our sister, who was only four, had no idea what was going on.

As soon as Dad left, he got an apartment ten minutes from our house. Every other weekend and on Tuesdays, he'd pick up the three of us and take us there. I had fun with Dad, especially after he got us our dog, Russell. But still, I couldn't believe my father wasn't going to move back home. I started thinking that if I had been nicer to him and Mom, all this wouldn't have happened.

Meanwhile, I had to get used to so many changes. The

first was Mom working full-time instead of just half a day as she had been. Although Grandma came to watch us, I wanted my mother and was angry when I couldn't have her. Besides, Grandma wasn't here all the time, so Mom hired baby-sitters in her place. With so many different people making the rules, we kids had no discipline. Soon the house was a wreck, with Logan and me leaving dirty dishes in every room.

At the end of the day, when Mom came home, she'd see the mess and yell. The next day Logan and I would go right back to doing the same thing. The sitters didn't know how to control us. This went on until three years ago, when Mom hired John, the baby-sitter who lives with us today. He came up with the idea of a "fine jar," which Mom agreed to. We would have to put money into a jar if we didn't clean up well, and Mom and John could use the money as they liked. When Logan and I heard this, we were astounded. It was the first time Mom had ever put her foot down.

Usually Mom let things slide, even when she was stressed and had so much to do. The hardest thing for her was trying to make a living. Almost immediately after Dad left, she began to work long hours, and over the years that hasn't changed. Today she's either busy in her downstairs office, helping students, or she's out of the house, teaching. On Tuesday and Thursday nights she's not home until nine-thirty. Most of the time John's with us, and we have fun playing Nintendo, but I miss my mother.

Since Mom's become a single parent, I don't get to see much of her. When I come in from school, she may be there, but she barely has time to say more than hello. Before you know it, her student is coming up the driveway, and she goes downstairs to work. If I have something to tell Mom, it has to wait until five-thirty when she comes out of her office to have dinner with us. We get about twenty minutes together but Logan and Dane are around, so there's no privacy. Then Mom rushes off to the next student.

Some nights, though, she's free. Then she helps me with my reading and social studies homework. Until last year I was in a special school program because I had so much trouble with those subjects, but now that I'm in sixth grade, the teachers say I don't need extra support. Still, I'm not reading at my grade level, and I get embarrassed when I make a mistake. But nothing embarrasses me more than when people find out that my parents aren't together. Although there are three kids in my class in the same situation, I try to keep it a secret.

When I was younger, it was even harder for me living with just Mom. We'd be out somewhere, and I'd have to go to the bathroom, but she couldn't take me into the men's room. Instead, she'd tell Logan to take me. My brother and I would walk through the door together, so nervous to be in a strange place.

Dane, being a girl, had it easier. Mom seemed more comfortable with her than with us boys. At bedtime Mom would give Logan and me quick good-night kisses, then go into Dane's room and talk to her for a long time. This made me jealous, and one day I told Mom how I felt. Now, at night, she spends more time with Logan and me in our room. Even then, I'm not totally alone with Mom. The only way it's just the two of us is when Dane and Logan visit friends. On those days Mom and I go off to play tennis or racquetball. But like in most families with a bunch of kids, this doesn't happen often.

About a year ago Mom gave Dane, Logan, and me our own house keys. Logan, who's in seventh grade, comes in first and is usually home when I get in from school. Unfortunately, we fight a lot because without Mom there, he thinks he should be in charge. Just because he's the oldest and the strongest, he has no right to declare himself the boss. He's not my father and he shouldn't act as if he is. I'm sure if Dad were living here, Logan and I would get along better, because Mom wouldn't have to work so much and Logan would have less responsibility.

Still, my brother and I are friends. When I get into trouble with Mom or Dane, he's the one I go to. Since we share the same room and are both interested in sports and collecting baseball cards, we have a lot in common.

Now that money isn't as big a problem for our family and we are old enough to help Mom in the house, there's time for the four of us to do more together. About once a month we meet with two of our friends' families and have a dinner party. One family brings hamburgers or pizza, another brings the dessert, and the third supplies the house. While the kids play, the mothers and fathers talk. No one cares that Mom's a single parent.

Luckily, Mom also enjoys hiking in the woods or playing a game of football. Since Dad moved to Florida a year ago, she's the only parent around to have fun with. I talk about this with Dad when he calls twice a week and tell him that it's not good that he lives so far away. He understands but says that's the way it has to be.

I miss Dad a lot and wish we could be together more, but I wouldn't want him living at home with us again. He and Mom didn't make a good couple. Right now I'm happy. My family situation is better than it used to be.

After watching Mom raise us by herself, I'm beginning to think it might be fun bringing up kids as a single parent. It would be hard dealing with the problems all alone, but I'd rather do that than get married and pick the wrong person. That sometimes worries me.

I'm lucky to have a mother who enjoys her kids. The way she acts, you'd never believe her life was difficult. She's managed on her own to make us a happier family.

*"I worry too much
about money."*

Dane,
age 10

As long as I can remember, things between my parents
weren't so good. When I was four, Dad was living in a
different part of the house, and he and Mom weren't
talking. We kids would hand him his mail and give him
messages from Mom.

The day he left, Mom told me he wasn't coming back,
but I didn't know what she was talking about. I thought
he must have gone for a walk. When nighttime came
and he wasn't there, I was worried. I told Logan, my
older brother, that maybe Dad had been kidnapped.
Logan, who was young himself, wasn't sure what was
happening.

Even when we three kids started visiting Dad in his

own apartment, I was confused. Every time I'd see him, I'd ask why he and Mom weren't together. He always avoided answering me. He doesn't like talking about serious things.

Since Dad left, he has hardly supported us kids, and that makes me angry. I know that right now he's waiting to pass the bar exam in Florida, where he lives, and he has to watch his money. But what about all the other years?

Without him giving child support, it's been much harder for us. When he lived here, we used to go to the movies or to restaurants, but we barely do that anymore. Now we have to conserve our money. When my pants wear out, we wait for sales to get new ones. And I can't buy as many earrings as my friends do, so instead, I make them. In a way, it's an advantage to be able to do these things on my own, and it keeps me from getting bored. But I worry too much about money.

Recently Logan started letting Sloan and me come along when he baby-sits. He shares what he makes with us, so now I have a little extra to spend. We're also putting up signs around the neighborhood to get jobs this summer. I hope someone needs us.

Since Mom and Dad's divorce, my brothers and I have become a lot closer. If we're upset about something or are having trouble with schoolwork, we go to one another for help. Probably if both our parents were at home, we would ask them first.

Although most of the week Mom works in her office

in the house, I don't get to see her that much because she's busy with her students. But if there's something important I have to tell her, she usually can find time for me. She never makes me feel I'm creating a big deal out of nothing. And she's good at keeping secrets. With her as the only parent at home, I don't have to worry that what I say will go further than the two of us.

Last year, before Dad moved to Florida, where my grandma and aunt have homes, he asked me if I wanted to live there with him. I told him no and said I was comfortable the way things were. I know Dad misses us kids. Although we speak to him twice a week, it's not the same as when we would see him every other weekend. Sometimes I think he might get too lonely and insist on joint custody. Then my brothers and I would have to split our homes for six months of the year. I like living with Mom and want to keep going to my school so I can be near my friends. All this is too much for a kid my age to think about.

Luckily, in my family we talk about what's going on, and I've spoken to a private therapist. A few years ago, when the divorce got real bad, I even went to the school psychologist and opened up about these personal things. But whenever I want to tell Dad how I feel, I usually clam up. Maybe it's because I don't want to hurt him since we're not living together. At the same time I'm angry that he moved so far away. I get jealous when I see a friend's father coach a team, and I wish it was my dad doing that. Then I remember that he didn't like doing that years back and probably wouldn't be involved in my sports even if he did live nearby.

With Dad no longer in the house, Logan has sort of taken over the fatherly role, especially if Mom and John, the sitter, aren't here. Logan cooks dinner—chicken, meat loaf, spaghetti—and he takes charge of telling Sloan and me what to do. He'll say, "Dane, clean your room" or "Take a shower before bed." While I don't like his bossiness, I'm happy I have him as an older brother. He takes care of me and makes me feel safe. It's nice to have him and Sloan to keep me company. Since the divorce, the three of us are a team. And with Mom, we make up our own family.

L. to r. Logan, Sloan, Dane

"I wanted a father so much."

Sakeeya, age 11

I'm not sure what the name Sakeeya means, but if I could choose, it would be "beautiful person." The only time I'm not so nice is in the morning when somebody wakes me.

From the day I was born, Mom raised me by herself. She raised my nine-year-old sister, Nakeeya, by herself, too. Nakeeya and I have different fathers. Mom wasn't married to either of them.

Over the years Mom has told me what our life was like when I was younger. She says that at the time she had me, she was working as a clerk-typist and earned enough to support the two of us. Then, right before Nakeeya was born, Nakeeya's father moved in, and soon

Mom quit her job to take care of my sister and me. A few months later Nakeeya's dad, who was on drugs, left. Although he still gave Mom money, it was too little for us to get by on, so we had to go on welfare. Some months we were so poor that we couldn't pay the rent or buy food. Then Grandpa would come over with groceries.

Mom hated being on welfare. She had grown up on welfare, and she had always been embarrassed by it. More than anything, she didn't want my sister and me to feel the way she had as a little girl. Mom also hadn't graduated from high school. She decided to get her high school equivalency diploma so she could find a good job. As soon as she earned the diploma, she applied to college and was immediately accepted.

All her classes were in the morning. While she was away, I went to kindergarten and Nakeeya went to a Head Start program. In the afternoon Mom worked as a teacher's aide in a day-care center, and a neighbor watched my sister and me.

At the end of the day I couldn't wait to see my mother. There was so much I wanted to tell her. But she'd always come in exhausted, and she didn't want to talk. Instead, she'd lie down and take a nap. The longer this went on, the angrier I got.

Meanwhile, our money problems were getting worse. The year I was seven and Mom was a college sophomore, we were so poor that we didn't have enough change to use the machines at the Laundromat. Every night we washed out our clothes to have something clean for the next day. Also our apartment then was so tiny that the three of us had to sleep in one room. And we lived in a bad neighborhood across the street from my school, where drugs were sold.

From all the stress, Mom became very tense and would yell and hit Nakeeya and me for no reason. I didn't understand why this was happening and began blaming myself for all the bad stuff. At that time I had been begging her for a talking Cabbage Patch doll, and I thought maybe that was causing our troubles.

Meanwhile, I hadn't seen or spoken to my father—who lived in a different state—since I was three. All through the years I kept wondering why he had disappeared from my life. Mom tells me that as a little girl, I wanted a father so much that when Nakeeya's dad lived with us, I thought he was my father and called him Dad. The year I was in second grade, he died. I cried and cried, thinking my real father was gone.

Now I felt that anyone who had a dad was better than me. Especially in third grade I had a difficult time, because that year most of my friends lived with two parents. I was so ashamed of my family situation that I made up stories about Dad coming to take me out for dinner. One day I wrote about this in the diary I handed in to my teacher. My teacher, who knew I lived only with Mom, called her to say she was concerned that I was fantasizing.

Immediately Mom brought me and Nakeeya to a counselor at a family service agency. Every week for the

next two years, the three of us went together and told
the counselor what was bothering us. I said that I was
unhappy because Mom wasn't spending enough time
with me, and we talked about it. Soon after, Mom promised to set aside a special day for Nakeeya and me, and
she said nothing would interfere with our plans. Since
then she takes us bike riding in the park, and when she
has extra money we eat at a restaurant.

Another thing I brought up with the counselor was
how much it hurt not having a dad. I told her and Mom
that I wanted to call my real father to let him know how
difficult it was for me without him around. They both
agreed this was a good idea, and Mom gave me his
telephone number. When Dad answered the phone, I
felt like I was talking to a stranger.

A few months later he came to visit. I couldn't believe
my eyes when I saw him. Here was my real father, tall
and handsome, standing in front of me. I had just had
my tonsils out, and he brought me ice cream to make
my throat feel better.

He stayed for two days and then went home. The rest
of the year we called and wrote to each other, and he
sent Mom money for Nakeeya and me. Even though
Nakeeya is not his child, he told her that she was now
part of his family.

This past summer Nakeeya and I visited him for two
weeks at his house, where his girlfriend and their two-
year-old child also live. We had the best time ever, pic-
nicking and going to the pool with Dad and his other

kids who live nearby. This coming summer Nakeeya and I are supposed to go out there to be with him again.

Last year Mom graduated from college and got a full-time job counseling college students. Finally we were off welfare, but we still had money problems. Within months the school where Mom worked had its budget cut, and for a while she had no job. Sometimes Nakeeya and I would find her crying and would feel so sad. To make her happier, I wrote cards telling her how much I loved her.

Today Mom is working again. Now she comes home with lots of papers from her job, which she has to go over for the next day. So once more that means she's tired a lot. At least Nakeeya and I are old enough to help her some nights by preparing dinner. We make hamburgers, french fries, chicken, and Jell-O.

We also share the house-cleaning with Mom and take the clothes to the Laundromat. For us, the Laundromat is fun because our friends are there, helping their moms, too. Like Nakeeya and me, they also live with a single mother who works full-time.

Since Mom has a better-paying job, we're able to live in a good area. We have an apartment that's large enough for each of us to have our own bedroom and to invite people for dinner on the holidays. For Thanksgiving, Grandpa and his wife, Judy—I call her Grandma—came over. Grandma brought a blueberry pie that she and I had baked together. On Christmas we went to her house, bringing delicious homemade

cakes and cookies that Mom, Nakeeya, and I had made.
Since Mom sees that Nakeeya and I are responsible
kids, she's given us our own house keys, so we don't have
to go to after-school day-care programs anymore.
Instead, we get home from school and do our homework, or if the weather's nice, we play outside. When
Nakeeya starts talking to other kids, I keep an eye on
her to make sure she's okay. Just like Mom protects me,
I protect my sister.

Some days after school Nakeeya and I visit our
friends. But before we can make any plans, we have to
tell Mom where we're going and promise to call her the
minute we get there. That way Mom knows we've arrived
safely. Later on, Mom calls the friend's house to make
certain we are at the place we said we'd be. With all the
crime around, I understand why Mom's concerned
about us, but I hate being checked on. When I tell her
how I feel, she listens but still won't budge. She's real
strict about whom we hang out with and about our ed-
ucation. Mom wants us kids to do well and not to get
labeled troublemakers.

But Mom really doesn't have to worry about me since
I do great in school and have gotten lots of achievement
certificates in math and science, my favorite subjects.
Twice a week I go to Project Uplift, a special after-school
program, to teach me even more. And I'm also busy
singing in the church choir. When I grow up I want a
job in communication arts so I can create games like
Nintendo.

This fall Mom is planning to start graduate school to become a social worker, and that will mean she'll have even less time for my sister and me. Then, more than ever, I'll wish there were two parents in the house. With just one it's impossible to get enough attention.

Even if Dad lived nearby, it would be better, but it looks like that will never happen. Instead, I have to be satisfied knowing he's a nice man who treats me well when we're together. I'm proud of him and Mom, too. I'm lucky to have a mother and father who make me feel good.

L. to r. Sakeeya, Nakeeya

"I don't mind living with just Mommy."

Nakeeya, age 9

Since I was born, I've lived with Mommy and my sister, Sakeeya. Mommy tells me that my daddy only lived with us for a short while. When I was four and a half, before I got to know much about him, he died. I have a picture of my daddy sitting in a red car. It would be nice to have a car like that. Mommy can't drive so we don't own a car.

Still, I don't feel cheated or different because I don't have a father. Most of my friends have no daddy either. When I go to their houses, I'm not reminded about families with two parents.

My friend Kiara lives with her mother and stepdad, and I don't see her family doing things differently from mine. Like us, they sit down to dinner together at night, and they celebrate holidays with relatives like we do. When Kiara needs clothes, her mommy takes her shopping the way mine does, and they play board games together the way Mommy, my sister, and I do. It doesn't seem so special in Kiara's house just because there's a mother and father there. So what's the big deal about having two parents?

But once in a while I'd like a father around to play kickball with or to wrestle. Mom and Sakeeya don't enjoy that kind of stuff. Still, I have fun with my sister. She's a nice person. We hardly fight.

Of all the people in my family, I think Mommy's the one who could use a man around the most. As a single parent, she has to work so hard. It's not easy raising two kids alone. In the morning she wakes us up early, makes sure we're dressed right for school, and gets us out of the house on time. Then she leaves for her job, where she has lots to do. Later on, when she comes home, she has to cook the dinner, if it's her turn, and get us to bed. Day after day it's the same thing for her. Sometimes I think she must be bored, with no grown-up in the house to talk to.

Now and then Mommy has to go to a conference, which can last three or four days. Because there's no father at home, she has to find someone to watch Sakeeya and me. Luckily, Grandpa lives nearby, so we stay at his house. He lets us walk the dog and takes us to Burger King.

Maybe one day Mommy will marry and have someone else to help her run the family. She dates a lot of nice men, but she hasn't found the right person yet, which means she'll probably be a single parent for a long time. If that happens, she'll have to keep working hard and will barely be free to play with me or answer my questions. This makes me mad. I want my mother to give me more attention.

When she graduated from college and got a full-time job, I thought we could do more together, but now she's too busy. And we're still not rich either, but I'm not complaining. Compared to homeless kids, I have a lot, including a grandpa who spoils Sakeeya and me. He bought us both new bikes when it wasn't our birthday. And on Easter, he gave me a stuffed teddy bear that was holding a real camera. It worked, and I took a picture of the family.

Every night, before I go to bed, I say my prayers and give thanks for having enough food and clothing, and for a grandpa who's so nice and a mommy who cares about me and my sister. I don't mind living with just Mommy. If I didn't have to see her struggle so much to raise Sakeeya and me, I think I would want to have kids as a single parent, too. The only problem is that with one parent earning all the money, I might not be able to afford a red car. That's what I really wish for. Maybe some day, if Mommy makes more money, we can get a car and go on long trips together.

*"Now that Mom's not here,
who's going to tell
Dad what girls like?"*

Ariel,
age 9

Until last year my twin brother, Robert, and I lived with our mother and father. Then one day, while Robert and I were in school, Mom suddenly died from a stroke. When Dad told us what had happened, we couldn't stop crying. That night and a few nights afterward, we slept with Dad in his big bed.

For the next two weeks Dad stayed home from his teaching job to get things in order. Right away he started interviewing baby-sitters, and finally he hired Rady, who now lives with us Monday through Friday. She cooks and cleans the house and is home when Robert and I come in from school.

Dad arrives at six in the evening, just as he always has,

and then we all sit down for dinner. Now instead of Mom making the meal, it's Rady who does it. The rest of the jobs that were Mom's have been taken over by Dad, plus he has his own work. Before, Mom used to drive us to school at eight-fifteen. Today Dad drops Robert and me off a half hour earlier than we need to be there so he can get to work on time. Until school begins, Robert and I hang out at the playground with other kids, or if the weather's bad, we sit inside.

On Saturdays too Dad drives us around, taking me to gymnastics and Robert to Sabbath services at the synagogue. On Sundays he does all the Hebrew school carpooling to make up for not helping during the week. I feel bad that Dad is the only one who can get us places. He has it worse than Mom did, because this year Robert and I are doing more activities.

To make sure Dad doesn't get too worn out, Robert and I pitch in at home on Rady's two days off, cleaning our rooms and taking turns clearing the table. Now that Dad's taught me how to work the washing machine, I sometimes do the laundry too, which I don't mind.

Whenever I can, I try to make it easier for Dad by doing things, like my homework, without having to be told. I'm also working hard on acting nicer to my brother. Before Mom died, Robert and I used to get into lots of fights, mostly over who got to use the remote control on the TV. But now I go out of my way to cooperate with my brother so Dad won't have to get in the middle of our arguments.

Because Robert and I have been fighting less, we've become closer. He no longer yells at me when I come into his room without asking. Instead, he tells me in a calm way to leave, and I listen without starting up.

But I miss Mom a lot and find it hard to get used to her not being here. We were very close. I trusted her more than anyone and would tell her the secrets my friends told me. It's not that I don't trust Dad. He's just not interested in the kind of stuff Mom and I enjoyed. He'd rather discuss sports with my brother than take turns reading aloud from a mystery book the way Mom and I would do. And he doesn't really understand girls.

A few years ago, when Mom was alive, I asked her if I could move out of my brother's room and take over the guest room, painting it pink, my favorite color. When she brought up the subject with Dad, he said no. But then Mom explained that I was getting older and needed my privacy, and finally Dad agreed. Now that Mom's not here, who's going to tell Dad what girls like?

When it comes to picking clothes, he has no idea what style I look good in. He'll suggest an outfit in a catalog that is definitely not for me. And it's worse when we go to a store, because then I have to go into the dressing room by myself and am left alone to make the decision.

Robert doesn't have these problems, since he and Dad are both males and have the same taste and interests. They love computer games and are involved in Boy Scouts. Dad is now the chairman of Robert's troop.

A few weeks ago I told Dad that he and I needed to find an activity we both enjoy, so the next time Robert went to a friend's house, Dad took me to Carvel. It was sort of special but not exactly what I was thinking of. I could have explained this to Dad, but I decided not to. He's got enough on his mind, and I don't want to make it more difficult.

But I did bring it up in the group Robert and I belong to with other kids whose parents have died. My counselor understood why I didn't want to hurt Dad's feelings, but she also told me that it's important to tell others what's bothering me. She said that when a parent dies, kids feel guilty for not having always been nice to that parent and sometimes try to act extra good with the one who's alive. I knew what she was talking about and am now trying hard to say what's on my mind.

While it's not been easy for me with Dad as the only parent in charge, I must admit that some changes he's made in the family are pretty good. For one, he takes Robert and me to Friendly's and McDonald's much more than Mom did. And we have fewer rules to follow. Although we still have to be in bed at nine o'clock on school nights, we can now keep our lights on longer to read, which Mom would never have allowed. Also, Robert and I have convinced Dad to let us stay up until nine-thirty instead of nine on weekends.

Dad's not that strict. He doesn't care much if we take a shower or two less a week or invite more than one friend at a time to the house. That kind of stuff isn't important to him. But like Mom, he wants to be sure the family stays close.

Since Dad's parents live nearby, we go to their house very often. And a few months ago we also flew to Florida to visit Mom's parents. It was Grandma's seventy-fifth birthday. At first it was hard seeing everybody, because we hadn't been together since Mom's funeral. Grandma, though, knew just how to make me feel more comfortable. She arranged for my three girl cousins and me to sleep in one bedroom and brought us lots of munchies.

Another thing that Dad's kept the same is how we observe the holidays. Although Dad is Christian, Robert and I were brought up Jewish, like Mom. Now that she's gone, we still celebrate Passover, going to Uncle Howie's house for the first seder and spending the second night with Mom's friend Barbara. On Chanukah Dad gives us gifts, and then he gives us some on Christmas too, which is how it always was. I'm glad he didn't change these things, because otherwise I'd feel so mixed up.

With all that's happened this year, it's been hard for me. Yet I'm proud of how well I've done. Even when I got bad grades in school, I was able to pull myself together and get them up by the next report card. And I've continued playing the piano, which I started years ago and still love.

Dad too seems happier and is now beginning to go out with new people. Just last week he asked a woman friend from work to come with us to see Robert's troop put on a magic show. From the way he looked, I think he liked her company.

I know it's hard for Dad without Mom, but there's no doubt he has fun with us kids. While there's nothing else in the world I'd want more than having my mother back, at least I have a dad who loves me a lot.

*"I feel uncomfortable
talking to Mom
about girls."*

Alex,
age 12

Dad was born in Peru and Mom in America. They met while they were both working in Brazil and got married there, and that's where my younger sister, Diana, and I were born. When I was four, Dad was offered a fellowship to a university in the United States. The university was in Rhode Island, where Mom had grown up and where Grandpa and his wife, Gina, and our other relatives on Mom's side of the family still lived.

Two months after we moved to Rhode Island, my parents separated.

While I've forgotten a lot about those times, I'll always remember the fighting that went on between my mother and father. Still, I didn't think their marriage would end.

But one day Dad moved out. Mom tells me he got his own apartment not far from our house and visited Diana and me one or two days a week.

From the moment he left, I became very quiet and didn't want to go outside and play with the other kids. Some of this was because I felt strange in a new country, but I also was sad. I missed my father. With my mother out looking for a job most of the day, there was only the housekeeper to take care of Diana and me.

After being in America for two years, Dad went back to Brazil, where he lives today. Now we only see each other once a year, in the summer, when he visits my sister and me for three weeks.

Over the years friends have come to my house and asked where my father is. I tell them he lives in Brazil because my parents are divorced. Usually they don't question me anymore, but still, I'm not sure if they really believe my story. So when Dad comes up in the summer, I go out of my way to introduce him to them.

For me, one of the hardest things about the divorce is that Dad's not around and Mom's not home that much either. As a single parent, she has to earn the money to support our family, and that means working long hours. Although she teaches and is done at three, she takes after-school courses and comes home late a few times a week. On those days Diana and I have to eat dinner without her.

At least when we lived in Rhode Island, we were near our relatives, but a year and a half ago we moved to another state. Now it's pretty much the three of us except for Mom's friend Christine. We see her once in a while.

When Mom's not home, I, as the oldest child, have the responsibility of being in charge of Diana and myself. Since I'm in junior high, my school lets out an hour before my sister's, and I come in first. If I know that Mom doesn't have an afternoon appointment, I'll go to the schoolyard and play basketball or baseball with friends. But if Mom's going to be away, I'll hang out with my sister. Depending on the weather, we'll play catch or we'll watch TV.

Years back, when Diana was real young, Mom would ask me to keep an eye on her while she went to the grocery. My sister would run off and disappear, which was scary. But now that Diana is older, she's pretty cooperative. She helps me get the dinner ready, and later we do the dishes together.

As the only male in the house, I kind of take my father's place. While I don't protect Mom or Diana, when Mom's not here, I'm still the one to remind my sister to do her homework instead of watching TV. Diana doesn't like me telling her what to do, but I feel that as her older brother, I'm better at deciding what's good for her.

For a brother and sister, Diana and I get along pretty well. If Mom's not home and Diana has had a bad day at school, I comfort her. As a seventh grader, I understand a lot of her school problems. Once in a while—although not that often—something big will upset her, and then Diana waits till Mom gets in to have a private, involved conversation.

Diana is very close with Mom and confides in her more than I do. Maybe it has to do with the two of them being women. If Dad were here, I'm sure he'd be the one I'd turn to the most.

Although he and I talk on the phone every other week and write letters to each other, it's not the same as having him here when I want to ask him a question. While Mom's real nice and will discuss subjects like sports with me, I feel uncomfortable talking to her about girls or how my body's changing. Sometimes I bring up these things with Peter, my Big Brother, during our weekly visit, but if it can wait, I hold it until the summer, when Dad visits. Then we two go off together and talk and talk.

Another problem for me about living with just Mom is that her friends are mostly single women without kids. Every time we visit them, I stick out. Except when I'm with my friends or my Big Brother, I'm usually in the minority. On holidays, though, we visit Grandpa and Gina, and then I'm not the only male around. Grandpa has two young sons, and with my four boy cousins who are visiting too, I feel great. The best part is that we all bring our baseball cards and spend half the day looking at them.

My friend Cliff's parents are also divorced. He lives with his father. Although his problems are different from mine, we sometimes talk about how it feels not to have two parents at home. Last year, when we first moved here, I also spoke to my guidance counselor—about school problems I was having, but not about my family. Now, since my grades are good and I behave well, we no longer meet. Still, I wish there were some special adult I could confide in. If the school formed a group for kids who lived with a single parent, I'd join. I've told Mom about this, and she said she'll look into it.

What worries me most is that one day Dad might decide not to visit my sister and me anymore. Since he lives with a girlfriend and their three-and-a-half-year-old child, I'm afraid he'll get involved with his new family's problems and forget about Diana and me. I've tried to convince him to move back to the United States so this won't happen, but he says he can't because of his job. He's a mathematician for the Brazilian government.

At least I know that Mom will always be here for me. She might not be at home as much as I'd like, but there's no chance that she'd ever leave Diana and me. I love her and I love Dad, too. Too bad she and Dad couldn't make it together.

Yet, in spite of their bad marriage, I want to get married someday and have kids. First, though, my number-one wish is to become a doctor who specializes in heart surgery and saves people's lives. Since my parents' smartness has rubbed off on me, I don't think this is impossible. My second wish is that I find a wife who is pretty, intelligent, and has a good sense of humor. Then we'll spend a long life together and live happily ever after.

Alex and Diana

*"I'm lucky to have
an older brother."*

Diana,
age 9

When I was one and a half, my parents separated, and two years later they divorced. Mom got custody of my older brother, Alex, and me, and since then we've lived together. Because I was so young when my parents' marriage ended, I can't remember ever living with both of them in the same house.

Now Dad's in Brazil and only comes up in the summer. At that time he gives Mom a little money to support us, but hardly enough, so Mom's the one who has to pay all the bills. Her job as an ESL (English as a second language) teacher in a high school earns her enough for us to get by, but we're not rich. A year and a half ago we had to move out of the house we were renting to one that cost less. Now we just have one bedroom, which Mom and I share. Alex sleeps in an alcove that Mom's blocked off with bookcases.

Compared to homeless people, we're okay, but I can't have a long phone conversation with a friend because it costs too much. Maybe one day I'll win the lottery, and then things will get easier for my family.

Right now Mom works hard, leaving the house early in the morning to get to her classes on time. Since there are no school buses where we live, she drops me off in front of my building before she goes to hers. I don't like this, because I have to wait around by myself for a half hour until the other kids get there. If I had two parents at home, I'm sure one would drive me to school at eight-thirty, when everyone else arrives.

At least Mom's home from work soon after I get into the house, except on days she has a course or meets a friend in the city. Then I stay with my brother, who gets home before me. With him there, I always have company.

If I can't do my math homework, Alex shows me how, because he's a math whiz. I do much better in reading and sometimes tell him the words he gets stuck on. Usually we get along well, except when I ask to borrow his Walkman or when he tries to take Dad's place.

On the nights Mom is out, he'll turn off a TV program I'm watching and tell me to do my homework. I know he's trying to prevent me from getting grounded by Mom, but I don't think this is a brother's job.

Mostly, though, he's a good baby-sitter. Whenever it's thundering and lightning and I get frightened, he comforts me. I'm lucky to have an older brother.

A few months ago my Girl Scout troop had a father-daughter dance, and my troop leader said that those kids who couldn't bring their dads should ask someone else they felt close to. One girl brought her uncle, and I invited Alex. We had a lot of fun, but I wished my father could have been there.

Although other kids in school live without a father, it still makes me feel funny. Maybe that's why I hang out with my friends Erika and Louisa, who are "dadless" like me. Louisa's dad died, and both of Erika's parents were killed in a car accident, so now she lives with her aunt and uncle. Erika and Louisa understand how I feel, and also they're nice kids.

It's hard for me with my dad living far away. Every time I hang up the phone after speaking to him, I cry; I miss him so much. Mom knows I'm sad then and holds me. She makes me feel better.

Still, she can't change certain things, like how embarrassed I feel when friends come to the house and I say, "Meet my mother and brother," instead of introducing them to my father. This summer when he comes up, I'm going to invite these kids over, so they can see I have a nice dad, too.

The best part about Dad is that he doesn't force me to do things. If he tells me to brush my teeth and I keep playing, he gently pushes me into the bathroom and makes a joke of it. He also doesn't care whether or not my bed is made or how I keep my room.

Next to Mom, he's easygoing. Mom's the one who makes me practice my viola regularly, while Dad never would, and she grounds me when I call my brother stupid. But Mom can be a lot of fun, too. If I had to pick one parent to live with, it would be her, because she's easy to talk to. At night she sits on my bed, and we talk about what's gone on in school. When I've had a hard day and am upset, she calms me down.

Another good thing about Mom is that when I show her how I look in a new dress or skirt, she pays attention and says, "Nice outfit." My father and my brother don't notice my clothes. They'd rather play soccer or talk men stuff with each other. If Dad lived at home, those two would probably always go off together.

Sometimes I try to imagine what it would be like with Dad and Mom in the same house. Since they still don't get along great, it might not be so good. If we were sitting at the dinner table eating spaghetti and I took another portion, Mom would say, "Diana, you've had enough." Then Dad would contradict her and say, "Spaghetti's good for you, Diana." Pretty soon they'd be having a big fight, and I'd have to yell, "Stop, you guys!"

More than anything, I hate when my parents argue. It worries me that maybe one day Dad will get tired of it all and stop visiting Alex and me. Then there would be no one to spoil us. Each summer he arrives with a pile of Christmas presents that he's saved to give us in person.

If I wasn't so busy with Girl Scouts, viola lessons, and dancing, my mind would always be on missing Dad. The last time he called, I told him how hard it is with him so far away. He said he's going to send me a tape every now and then, so I can hear his voice more often. In the meantime we write to each other, although lately I've gotten a little lazy. Too bad my parents didn't know how to stop their fighting and had to get divorced.

I love Dad and I love Mom, too. Yet I'm glad I have Mom as my single parent. She understands more what it's like to be a girl and that's important to me.

"I'd rather live with Dad than with two parents who are always yelling."

Jason, age 9

When I was a baby, my mother and father adopted me, and until I was four, I lived with both of them. Then they separated. Meanwhile, they were planning to adopt another baby, Monique, who was also living with us when Dad left.

Now Dad tells me that he thought the separation would only last a week or two. But it didn't work out that way.

At that time Dad was working with troubled kids who lived away from home, in a special school. While Monique and I stayed with our mother in the new house Dad and Mom had bought together, he took a room at the school. Week after week he'd come to visit Monique and me, but Mom wouldn't let him see us.

Some days he'd arrive with groceries and she'd tell him to leave them at the door. This went on for eight months.

I was so young when this was happening. I had no idea why Dad wasn't at home. I remembered my parents fighting a lot, but I couldn't understand why I wasn't allowed to be with my father. From the way my mother acted, I knew she was very angry with Dad and with me, too. Every time I made a little mistake, she'd yell and hit me. Even today, I'm not sure what was bothering her.

Finally she told Dad she wanted a divorce. He agreed but said not until he was allowed to visit me. The first time we were together, he explained what was going on and asked, "Who do you want to live with?" It wasn't hard for me to decide. Immediately I pointed my finger at him and answered, "You!" In the end Dad got custody of me.

Once Dad was in charge of me, he had to find a place for us to live, because the school where he worked wouldn't let kids, besides the ones enrolled there, live on campus. For the six months it took until he got an apartment, I stayed with my aunt and uncle and their kids. Dad visited us on weekends. Since I had fun with these cousins and liked my aunt and uncle, I didn't mind being there, at least not in the beginning. The only hard part was when Dad came up for two days and then had to leave. I hated saying good-bye to him, because I was afraid that I'd never see him again. Before he'd drive off, we'd sit in the car and I'd hold on to his arm, crying for him not to go.

The longer we lived apart, the more I missed him and the more confused I got. In school, I became very quiet and wouldn't take part in activities. One day my teacher called Dad to tell him this. She recommended that I repeat the year. Dad said he thought my problems were caused by all the changes I had been through. He felt that once we got settled in our own place, I'd do better.

That summer he found us an apartment. Although moving meant I would have to make new friends and go to a different school, I felt it was no big deal. I was just happy to be with my father. To celebrate, he went out and bought me toys, books, clothes—everything I could ever want.

But soon after, I started acting out, breaking my toys and ripping my books. This really puzzled Dad. He couldn't figure out why I was so unhappy and brought me to a therapist. I was six at the time.

Together, Dad and the therapist watched me play in a room full of toys. Later the two of them talked. The therapist taught Dad ways to calm me down and make me feel safe. One thing the therapist suggested was that Dad just give me a single toy at a time so I wouldn't be overwhelmed. Dad followed what the therapist told him, and after four months, he saw a big change in me. So we stopped going to the therapist's office.

Now Dad and I have been together for over three

years. During this time he's changed jobs a lot, and that's meant we've had to live in different places. Today he removes asbestos and is also going to school to learn how to improve the environment. When he gets his certificate at the end of the summer, we'll be on the go again. This doesn't make me happy, because now that I'm older, I've made good friends and I'll miss them. Other than my friends, I'm not close to that many people.

The aunt and uncle I used to live with moved to Hawaii, so I don't get to visit them. And I only see my other aunt and uncle in the summer, because they live seven hours away. Except for my grandmother, who's nearby, and Dad's friend Uncle Leroy, it's just my friends and Dad. At Christmastime it gets lonely, because my grandmother takes a vacation then, so Dad and I are by ourselves. While I like decorating the tree with him and giving each other presents, it would be more fun if there were other people in my family.

Still, I'd rather live with Dad than with two parents who are always yelling. And when I compare myself to some of my friends who have a mother and father at home, I see that my dad and I spend more time together than they do with their parents. A couple of evenings a week, after he's finished with work, Dad and I swim at the gym pool or rent a movie. Other times we go walking downtown and he buys me ice cream.

Every night during the week Dad and I have dinner together at my grandmother's house. I go there straight from school, and later he comes. Before I'm allowed to play outside, Dad has made the rule that I have to finish my homework.

While I'm glad to be living with just Dad, I still wonder what it would be like to have a mother at home. Since most of the kids I'm friends with live with both of their parents, it hurts that my mother isn't around. Sometimes when I go to a kid's house and his mom offers me a drink and cookies, I start thinking that it must be nice having a mother there. But if the mother fights with the father, like mine did, then it's better to be living with just a dad.

Since Dad got custody of me, I hadn't seen or heard from my mother until last week, when Uncle Leroy brought her to our house as a surprise. When I saw her, I had no idea who she was.

The two of us went outside and talked about school and Monique. She told me that Monique still lives with her.

After half an hour, my mother left. I was confused. I didn't know when I'd see her again or if I wanted to.

Yet I wouldn't mind if Dad remarried somebody else one day. In fact, there was a woman he had dated for a long time, and I thought she was going to be the person he'd pick. She was okay, except that whenever she came to the house, Dad would talk and talk to her and forget about me. When they broke up, I wasn't that sad.

Now Dad isn't seeing anyone in particular and he doesn't seem to care. Maybe he's satisfied just living with me and feels it's not that hard being a single parent.

With me doing errands for him and him making enough money for the two of us, we do all right together. I'm going to make him something very special for Father's Day.

Watching Dad makes me think that it isn't that difficult for him to be raising me on his own. Although I don't ever want to get married, maybe I will adopt a little boy and bring him up by myself. We'll keep each other company and have lots of fun. If the kid is happy, he won't care that he's not living with two parents. But if he has to move all the time the way I have, he won't like that. Living with one parent wouldn't be that bad if I didn't have so many changes in my life.

Jason with his father

"No matter how tired Mom is, she has energy for my brother and me."

Meqhan, aqe II

It's been almost a year that my brother, Andy, and I have been living with Mom. Before that we were in Wisconsin with our dad and Jan, our stepmother. When I was one and a half and Andy was a year older, our parents divorced, with Dad getting custody of the kids. Mom was an alcoholic, so Andy and I and our two older brothers, Chris and Kevin, couldn't live with her.

Since Dad traveled during the week for business, he wasn't around to take care of us. My brothers went to live with our grandparents, where Dad stayed on weekends, and I went to live with my cousins Dixie and Tom, who were married but had no children. Dixie was real nice and had a dog. With her and Tom, I felt like I was part of a regular family.

During these years I saw my brothers on Saturday or Sunday and Mom visited me once a week. When I was four, she moved out of state, and from then until I was seven, we only got together at Christmas.

The year I was five, Dad married Jan. She had two sons—David, who's three years older than me, and Mike, who is Andy's age. Just before the wedding, we all moved into Dad's new house.

From the beginning it was obvious that Jan didn't like my brothers and me. She'd scream and hit us for no reason. She wasn't much better with her own kids. To make it worse, the kids fought with one another, too.

The only pleasant memories of family I have are when Dad would sometimes play baseball with us on weekends or would let me hold his tools while he repaired the plumbing. Aside from that and going to Grandma's for lunch after church on Sundays, my life was miserable.

Two years after Dad remarried, Mom went into treatment for alcoholism and stopped drinking. That summer my brothers and I spent two weeks with her, going hiking, swimming, and sightseeing in the city. When it came time to say good-bye, I didn't want to leave.

Meanwhile, my life at Dad's wasn't getting better. At least my older brothers were allowed to go off by themselves, but Andy and I had to hang around the house with Jan always there. It got so bad that the two of us talked about running away.

Finally, when we four kids came to visit Mom last summer, Andy and I told her we couldn't take it at Dad's anymore. She talked to us all to decide what we should do. Chris and Kevin, who are teenagers, said they wanted to live with Dad to be near their friends. But Andy and I told Mom we wanted to stay with her. Then Mom called Dad, and after a long discussion, he agreed we could be with her for one year, if she supported us.

At first I was so happy to get away from the craziness at home that I didn't mind being cramped up in Mom's one-room studio apartment, over a garage. She had fixed it up real pretty, so it wasn't that bad, even though the only private place was the bathroom.

But when school started, suddenly I became terrified that kids would find out I lived in a shack. I was sure that if I invited them over, they'd never want to be friends with me. Instead, I stopped talking to people in class unless they spoke to me first and spent most of my time daydreaming.

Mom saw how unhappy I was and she tried to get me to confide in her. But I wasn't used to trusting anyone and wouldn't tell her a word. Mom, though, was very patient and didn't force me. After a while of her talking softly and holding me, I started to open up little by little. Sometimes I told her about problems I was having in school, but mostly I spoke about what had gone on at Dad's. Mom listened and now and then gave me suggestions on how I might feel better.

Meanwhile, without our stepbrother Mike around to gang up with, Andy stopped teasing me. Soon we became sort of close, telling each other how we felt about living with Mom. For one thing, Andy suspected she was a lesbian because she had gay friends and went to gay meetings. He decided to come right out and ask her, and she said it was true.

All the while I had thought that Mom didn't date men because she wanted to devote her time to my brother and me. She said that my thinking on that part was right, but she added that if she did go out, it would be with women. When I heard that, I was embarrassed. I feel that it's up to Mom to do what she wants, but I don't want my friends to know about her life. In fact, I haven't even mentioned it to the therapist I've been seeing for the past six weeks. And I'm not ready to bring up the subject with Mom either. Still, I wouldn't trade being with her for the world. Too many good things have happened since we've been together.

The first was five months ago, when we moved from our one-room apartment to a large house we rent with Mom's friends Mo and Ruth. Now I have my own room and plenty of space. What's really special is that with these friends, we're like a family. Although Mo isn't here much because of his job, Ruth, who teaches, is home a lot and sits down to dinner with us every night. Sometimes she takes Andy and me to the movies and for ice cream.

Because Mom sometimes doesn't earn enough from her artwork, Ruth splits the grocery bills with her, even though she's one person and we're three. She also buys Andy and me clothes. Having her in the house is a definite plus. Without her pitching in, it would be harder for Mom as a single parent.

Of all things I think Mom worries most that she won't make it financially and then Andy and I will have to go back to Dad. This thought scares Andy and me and is something we talk about a lot. But just two weeks ago Dad called to say that he and Jan are getting divorced, so maybe now he'll let us stay here and he'll pay the child support.

I really want to keep living with Mom. She gives me so much attention. A few months ago she bought me gerbils, which we're breeding and selling to the pet store. I'm in charge of feeding the animals and cleaning their cages, and Mom checks in on them and gives them treats while I'm at school. Last week two albinos—gerbils with white coats and pink eyes—were born. Albinos are rare and they bring in more money. If we're lucky, we'll be able to raise more albinos.

Mom also bought me a ferret I've named Isis, after a Greek goddess. She got one for herself too, and one for Andy. And we have a dog. At Dad's we had a dog and a cat, but they were family pets, not animals that each of us was responsible for.

What amazes me is how much Mom has done for us on her small salary. We get an allowance, and I also take horseback-riding lessons every Saturday as part of a special program where Mom gives a donation instead of paying a lot each time. Somehow, she always finds ways to make things work out.

No matter how tired Mom is, she has energy for my brother and me. At night she'll read us fairy tales or play a game of cards with us. I love these times.

Yet I wish there was a dad around, too. While Andy says he's the man of the house, it's not the same as having a father who repairs the leaky pipes and fixes the steps.

Now that I've been living with Mom for almost a year, I've noticed that I'm changing. In the beginning I did terribly in school, but today my grades are getting better. Also, instead of going to soccer and Girl Scouts in the afternoon, I now prefer to read and draw. Mom says I'm a good artist, which may be true, but I think I'm a better horseback rider. When I'm older, I want to own horses and be a vet.

I doubt I'll ever get married after what went on between Dad and Jan and knowing that Mom and Dad couldn't make it either. Yet I like kids. Maybe if I got a good job and could manage the money situation, I would consider raising them as a single parent.

In the meantime I've got plenty of other stuff to worry about. Number one is, Will I be able to stay with Mom? Number two is to be happy and have lots of friends. If the first works out, then the rest probably will, too. In a few months I should know the answer.

*"I can't think of anything
I wouldn't tell
my mother."*

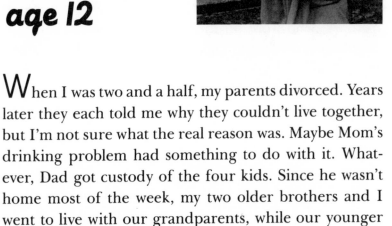

Andrew,
age 12

When I was two and a half, my parents divorced. Years later they each told me why they couldn't live together, but I'm not sure what the real reason was. Maybe Mom's drinking problem had something to do with it. Whatever, Dad got custody of the four kids. Since he wasn't home most of the week, my two older brothers and I went to live with our grandparents, while our younger sister, Meghan, stayed with Dad's cousin Dixie.

I liked living with Grandma and Grandpa. Grandpa was sickly, but he still was very nice. And Grandma was real special. When she found out I was taking care of abandoned baby rabbits, she cut up vegetables so they'd have something to eat.

The year I was six, Dad met Jan, and soon they got married. Jan had two sons, David and Mike. Mike was my age, and we hung around together, mostly getting in trouble by being mean to Meghan and starting fights with the other brothers. In our house, there wasn't a moment of peace. Jan constantly yelled and hit the kids, and Dad was very strict, always reminding us how to behave.

Because Dad traveled all week, we were more like a single parent household than a two parent one. With Jan in charge, it was sheer hell. Finally last summer it got so awful that I told Mom that if I couldn't live with her, I'd run away. Meghan felt the same. Our older brothers, who were on their own a lot, wanted to stay in Wisconsin. After talking and talking, Dad and Mom worked out an agreement.

In the beginning I was relieved to hear that I would be living with Mom. But soon the anger I had kept inside me for so long started erupting. If I saw my sister and Mom doing something special together, I'd freak out. I'd think, How dare Meghan get all the attention! In a rage, I'd break whatever I could get my hands on. Mom would try to prevent me from destroying things but she wasn't always successful. So she'd wait until I calmed down and then would take me into the bathroom, the only private place in the apartment, where she'd hold me and keep saying I was safe with her. It took me a while to believe her, especially when she said, "I'm going to love you no matter what."

Once I started confiding in her, I noticed she listened

and respected my point of view. She never acted like a boss just because she was the parent in charge. Even now, when we don't agree, she hears what I have to say before making a final decision.

After I had lived with Mom a while, I realized she didn't date and thought maybe she was cutting off that part of her life to give Meghan and me all her attention. Then I saw that most of the people she hung out with were gay, so I put two and two together and came right out and asked her if she was gay, too. She said yes.

At first I was embarrassed to think of my mother that way, but now I've accepted it. I've even gone to watch her march in a gay parade. Ruth and Mo, who share the house with us, are gay too, and that's been no problem. Still, I'm not comfortable telling kids about Mom because it's a personal subject. I can talk to my best friend, Jared, about a million things, but not about that.

Jared lives with both of his parents, yet they spend much less time with him than Mom, who's so busy trying to make a living, spends with Meghan and me. Even though Mom works late into the night making party decorations for weddings and Bar Mitzvahs, she finds ways to be with us. Still, when she's under real pressure, she gets stressed and that makes me sad. Recently I told her I could help her, and she thought that was a great idea. Now we work together and she pays me five dollars an hour. It's a lot of fun arranging the centerpieces, except it can be a drag when it's four in the morning and we're still not done.

As the only male around here—Mo's away a lot on

business—I'm the man of the house, otherwise known as the family "fix-it." If the tape recorder doesn't work or the VCR needs adjusting, I'm the one in charge, since I'm good at electronics and I enjoy repairing things. Of course, if a father were home, I'd let him take over the jobs, because I think that's what a dad should do instead of a child.

While I'm very happy being with Mom, I still wish my family were a more normal one, with two parents living together. Then I'd have a father to take me fishing and to baseball games. It may sound sexist, but I think most women don't like that sort of stuff, or wrestling either. Sometimes I wonder if I might be better off if my brothers lived with us, but we'd have to learn to get along better for that to work.

Anyhow, wishing for more males around is not important compared to worrying about whether Mom as a single parent will be able to support us. Right now we're hanging on by a thread and that makes me nervous. If we can't afford to pay the rent for this house, we'll have to move in with some of Mom's other friends. It won't be that terrible, but I'd rather it didn't happen.

For a kid my age, I've got a lot on my mind, and the difficulties still go on. Most people who meet me don't realize how hard it's been. Even though my life has gotten much better this year, I still have trouble keeping my mind on my schoolwork and have already failed a few courses. While I'm supposed to be smart, I probably will have to go to summer school unless my grades go up, which I think is beginning to happen.

Six weeks ago Mom arranged for me to talk to a therapist. She and Meghan go too, separately and to different people. Except for a time at Dad's when I was part of family counseling, I've never had anyone private to speak to. Now I feel comfortable confiding in the therapist, and I'm also very close to Mom. I can't think of anything I wouldn't tell my mother. Even when we lived apart and hardly saw each other, we always made the best of the time when we were together. Today with just Meghan and me at home, Mom can concentrate on us more. A few months ago she taught me how to play the guitar, and today we improvise and play songs with Meghan accompanying us on the piano.

She's also helped me to become more confident in myself and proud of my individuality. I no longer worry what other people think about my hairstyle or the clothes I wear. What concerns me, though, is that they'll find out I'm very sensitive and then push me around. So in school, I put on a tough act. Luckily, I have a few friends who know the real me. I can go to them if I have a problem.

Right now my main wish is to have my brothers here, so they too can get the best from Mom. But that won't happen unless Mom earns enough to keep us together. While some people want big cars and huge homes, I would just like my family to live under the same roof without fighting and worrying about money.

*"I'm just happy
not to stick out."*

Jessica,
age 8

Since I was born, it's been just Mom and me, and now our cat, named Happy. Way before Mom had me, she had been married for a short time and then got divorced. For years she felt bad because she wanted a child but hadn't met anyone she loved enough to be the baby's father. When she was thirty-five, she found out about artificial insemination. That's when the seed of a man is put inside the woman to make a child.

Mom then went to her doctor and told him she'd like to have the operation. The doctor, who had known Mom for years, carefully picked the man who would give her his seed. He was a doctor too, young, healthy, musical, and the same religion as my mother.

When Mom told my grandparents she was pregnant, they were so happy. Mom was their only child, and since she was getting older and wasn't married, they were afraid they'd never have grandchildren. Now what they wished for was happening.

The day I was born, Grandma and Papa were waiting in the hospital. They had flown up from Florida, where they lived, to be near Mom. The minute they heard the news about me, they screamed. Finally they had a grandchild.

Although I was too young to remember any of this, Mom has told me the story again and again. My favorite part is how Grandma and Papa acted. For a long time I didn't understand the rest. When I was four years old, I asked Mom why I had no dad, and at six, I tried to figure out how Mom could have had me without a man. Now that I'm older, I'm less confused by artificial insemination, but I have other stuff on my mind, like who could my dad be? Whenever I see a man with blue eyes walking down the street, I wonder, Is that my father? because I'm the only one in the family with eyes that color.

Kerry, one of my best friends, lives with just her mother because her parents are divorced. Sometimes her father doesn't visit when he's supposed to, and she tells me how mad that makes her. I say to Kerry, "You should at least feel lucky to have a dad, any kind of dad—except a child abuser. I don't even know who my father is."

Before Papa died last year, I thought of him as my substitute father. Although he lived in Florida and I didn't see him that much, he always made me feel special. I was Papa's little girl. Every time we were together, he read me stories and we played our favorite card game, Casino. Papa gave me lots of hugs. Because Mom's an only child, I have no uncles except for my grandparents' very old brothers. Other than Papa, there were no men in the family to kid around with me.

Lots of times I've told Mom how much I miss having a male around the house, and I think that's why she started inviting her friend Mitchell over. She used to go out with him, but now they're just friends. When he visits on weekends and the three of us go bowling or to the aquarium, I walk in between him and Mom and hold their hands. It makes me feel like I'm with a mother and a father.

Sometimes Mitchell teases Mom about how hard she tries to be both the man and woman of the house. A few weeks ago she spent eight hours putting together a bookcase and was so proud of her work until she realized the sides were on backward. After she finally straightened it out, she showed it to Mitchell. He joked that it would fall apart as soon as she put a book on it.

It must be hard for Mom to be a mother and father to me, especially on the nights I fall asleep on the couch and she has to carry me into my bed. I'm not that light! And while all my friends' mothers stay home and take care of the house, Mom's out working so we'll have enough money. She's a junior high school reading teacher and, lucky for me, gets home the same time I do. First we have a snack, and then she helps me with my homework. If it's nice outside, we go to the park, but if it's rainy or cold, we stay inside and play checkers or gin rummy.

The best part about Mom is that she's not pushy like some of my friends' moms and dads, who tell them they have to work real hard so that one day they can go to a famous college or get a big job. When I don't do that well in school, all Mom does is talk to me about how I can improve. I start thinking that it's not so bad just having a mother, particularly one like mine.

Also, because she has only me, I get a lot of attention. We're sort of pals, going on vacations together to places like England, where I got to ride a double-decker bus and see a bunch of castles. In the house too, we're a team, with me helping Mom change the ceiling light bulbs and clean up the place. The schedule Mom has made keeps us organized. I'm in charge of my room, mopping the kitchen floor until it sparkles, and spraying under the counters to get rid of the bugs. Also, I help Mom wash and wax the car and carry up the groceries. Some kids might complain about all this work, but I say to myself, It's *our* house.

Unless one day Mom gets married, she and I will probably always be very close. But if she finds a husband, then those two will become magnetized, and I won't have her alone as much. That might be hard for me to get used to. It makes me wonder if I'm better off without a dad in the house.

Yet when school discussions come up about families, I want a dad so bad. Not only is it embarrassing to tell people that my aunts and uncles are all in their seventies, and the cousins my age are my great-aunt's grandchildren, but I also have to explain how I was born. That especially gets on my nerves. Sometimes I tell kids, "Don't bother me. Go ask your mother about artificial insemination."

Since no one else in school was born the way I was, at times I feel so alone there. But when Mom takes me to a meeting of Single Mothers by Choice, which now has four hundred members, I meet other kids who were born the way I was. I feel better knowing I'm not the only one.

Not long ago I joined a school group for kids who live with a single parent. While most of the kids come from divorced families, it doesn't matter to me. I'm just happy not to stick out.

The other day the counselor who runs the group asked the kids what worried us most about living with one parent. I said I worried about losing my mom, and I remembered the day she went on a bus trip with my grandma and great-uncle. The bus was late, and she didn't return at the time she was supposed to. Although I had a baby-sitter, I panicked. I thought something tragic had happened to Mom. Nothing the baby-sitter did could stop me from crying. Maybe if I had a dad,

I wouldn't have been so scared. At least then there would be somebody left to take care of me.

Now and then I pretend I have a father and imagine what he'd be like. In my mind, he'd be cute and have blond hair like mine. On holidays he'd take me to his office to show me around, and when my friends came to the house, he'd joke with them. My dad would be the greatest in the world!

But having a father might mean more rules at home. Now if I lie to Mom, the worst thing she does is not let me watch TV, which isn't so terrible. But what if I had a dad who was real strict? Or one who didn't think I was so funny when I joked around? Then I'd be much quieter and more serious than I am. Still, kids are better off with a dad, even a strict one, than with none at all.

Right now I'm not sure if Mom will ever remarry. Once in a while she dates and introduces me to the men, but I don't think she's serious about anyone. Too bad, because I think it's good to have a man in the house. One day I'd love to get married and have children. When they were old enough to understand, I'd tell them how Mom had me, although it would be embarrassing.

Mom says that she hopes when I'm grown up, I won't be angry with her because she chose artificial insemination. I tell her that won't happen. What's most important is that I was born, and I'm glad about that. Although I get a funny feeling when I think of the way Mom created me, I'm still very happy to be alive!

"I was sure kids would laugh if they heard I lived with just one parent."

Vanessa, age 12

When I was four, Mom, who was divorced, came down to Chile and adopted me. She was the first mother I ever knew because the one who had given birth to me in Chile left my twin brother and me with our grandparents soon after we were born. For the next three years we stayed with our grandparents, until they could no longer take care of us. Then I was sent to live temporarily with another family until Mom came for me. I think my brother went to an aunt's. It was the last time he and I ever saw each other.

Although Mom explained in Spanish, the language I spoke at that time, that she was going to be my mother now and was taking me to another country, I had no idea what she was talking about. I thought she meant she was just taking me to a park. The moment we landed in America, I realized I was in a strange place and cried that I wanted to go back to Chile. It took me about two years to understand I was with Mom for good.

Almost immediately after I started living with her, people asked why we didn't look alike and where my father was. Whenever I could, I tried to avoid answering them, especially if kids were questioning me. Since most of my friends had a mother and father, I was sure kids would laugh if they heard I lived with just one parent. I felt different enough because of my adoption, but not having a dad made it worse. Despite my trying to keep my family situation a secret, in fourth grade, the truth somehow came out. Since then I've not hidden the fact that I'm adopted or that it's just Mom and me. Yet I'm not thrilled when people find out.

Today I'm sort of used to living with a single parent, even though I still would love to have a father. I know exactly the kind I'd want—one who hugs, kisses, and likes to horse around. When I was much younger, Mom dated a man named Elliot, and I made believe he was my real father. I called him Dad, even though Mom insisted they were just good friends. Now she's not dating much, so it looks like there will never be a dad around here, and that makes me sad. I'd like a father, because then I'd get more attention and I'd have somebody to keep me company when Mom isn't available.

The other night I asked her to play a board game

with me, and she said she wanted to read. If I had a dad or even a brother or sister, there'd be someone else for me to do things with.

Some days more than others can be pretty lonely, and Mom as an only child understands this. That's why she says it's important for us to make plans to be with people on weekends. Either we visit her friends or our cousins or I go to the movies with kids from school. If it were always Mom and me, we'd get on each other's nerves.

Once a week I meet with a bunch of girls my age to talk about subjects that are making us feel rotten. It could be parents, boys, or problems with a friend. Mostly I listen and try to help the others rather than let them know what's bothering me. I'm usually not comfortable sharing personal stuff with anyone other than Mom. Although, recently Mom took me to an adoption meeting and I started speaking to a fifteen-year-old girl there who has the same coloring as I. We talked about how hard it is to not look like our parents, and afterward, I felt better knowing I'm not the only one upset by this.

My life hasn't been easy, yet because of that, I've become more sensitive to other people who are also having it hard. When I see the homeless on the street, I want to do something to make them feel better. I also go out of my way to comfort the first and second graders I work with as part of community service. If one of them falls down and is hurt, I try hard to get the kid to laugh. One day I hope to be a doctor, and then I'll be able to help people even more. I've already started practicing, by bandaging Mom's leg after she had minor surgery.

The more I think about it, the more I feel that living with a single parent isn't the worst thing in the world. Mom makes me feel safe and has given me a good home. While I think it would be more fun with a father in the house, Mom and I have a good time, too.

Vanessa with her mother

"In my mind, kids are supposed to have a mother, too."

Todd,
age 10

For the past three years it's been Dad and me living together. This is the second time we've been in that situation. The first was after Tina, my mother, died in childbirth. Seven years later, Dad and Wendy, his second wife, divorced.

Right after Tina died, Dad and I moved to Illinois to be near Grandma, Grandpa, and Aunt Mary, who are on Dad's side of the family. They took care of me while Dad, who is a photographer, worked. When I was three, Dad decided we should go back to the state where I was born because the photography business was better there. Soon he met Wendy, and the next year they were married.

From the start I liked Wendy and called her Mom, because she was sort of a mother to me. Then one day, when I was seven, Dad told me they were getting divorced. I wasn't totally surprised, since the two of them were always yelling at each other. I hated hearing them fight and would go into my room and blast the TV to drown out the racket they made.

Still, I was sad to see Wendy go. Now who would be there when Dad wasn't home? At this time more than ever, I wished Grandma and Grandpa were nearby.

As it turned out, Dad arranged for me to go to a babysitter's house after school. And the following year he gave me my own house key, to make life easier for both of us. But from the beginning I did not like being alone. Every time I'd hear a strange noise in the apartment, I was sure it was robbers coming to take me. Even today, as a fourth grader, I'm not completely comfortable with no one else here. The minute I come home, I call a friend or turn on the TV to take my mind off scary things.

More than once I've asked Dad if I could invite a kid from school to keep me company, but Dad says that wouldn't be a good idea because we might get too wild and hurt ourselves.

Although I have plenty of friends whose mothers are home in the afternoon, I can't visit these kids, because they live too far away. While the mothers drive, they don't like picking up other people's children. If there weren't so much traffic on the streets, I'd bike over, but with all the cars, it's not safe. Luckily, most days Dad's home about an hour after I am. The second he walks through the door, I feel more relaxed.

Fortunately, in our apartment house, there's a couple named Diane and Paul, who share a business with Dad, taking wedding pictures on the weekend. We four have become so close that I think of Diane and Paul as family. On my last birthday Diane made a special dinner and we had a cake. Since she mainly works at home during the week, I sometimes stay with her if I'm sick and Dad can't get the day off. But if I have a dental appointment or need a haircut, it's Dad who takes me. He even comes home from work early to get me to my basketball games on time.

With no mother in the family, Dad has the job of two parents. I try to help him by doing some of the chores Wendy did plus carrying his photography equipment to the car, yet it's not much compared to what he does. Besides his weekend job, he is a medical photographer at a hospital. Along with all that, he shops for the groceries, makes dinner, and cleans the apartment. On his one day off he tries to give me attention by taking me to the library to get books for my school reports or playing ball with me in the park.

Depending on the season, the two of us might also go to the zoo or to a baseball game. I love doing special things with Dad. But now that he has two jobs, we don't have as much time together.

Hardest is when he has to photograph a wedding on

Saturday or Sunday and Diane and Paul have plans, too. Then I usually have to sleep at a friend's house, which is fun but makes me feel like I'm being shipped around. Dad knows how I feel and is not happy about this either, but he says there's not much else we can do right now. So I'll know he's thinking of me while he's on a shoot, he always brings me back a piece of wedding cake.

While Dad and I do a lot together, I still feel that living with a single parent isn't that great. Maybe if the rest of my family were close by—we have to take a plane to see them—I'd feel that my life was more like other kids' lives. And there would be people to spoil me. Although Dad buys me plenty of toys and I have a TV, a stereo, and an iguana in my room, that's not the kind of spoiling I'm talking about. I want somebody to be home at the end of the day to play Monopoly with me, a grandma to bake brownies with, and a grandpa to sit and watch sports with.

Since it doesn't look like any of this will ever happen, I wish at least there was a mother here, so I wouldn't have to explain to kids why I'm living with only a dad.

Last year a teacher recommended I join a school group led by a counselor for kids who live with single parents. Once a week for the next seven weeks, we met and wrote or talked about our feelings. It was the first time I ever told anyone how angry I was with Dad and Wendy for breaking up. After sharing this I felt a lot better.

Until recently I saw Wendy about every month, and

we'd go for lunch together and to the movies. But now weeks have gone by, and she hasn't come to visit. I know she likes me, and I can't understand what's going on. I miss Wendy, especially at bedtime, when she used to read me stories and kiss me good-night. Dad kisses and hugs me then, but it's not enough. In my mind, kids are supposed to have a mother, too.

Since Dad is dating again, he sometimes invites women to the house to have dinner with us. The best is when they bring their kids along. If I like the kids, I start thinking how great it would be to have a stepbrother or sister.

When I'm older and finish college, I plan to get married and have a child—just one, in case I have to raise the kid alone. If that happened, I'd follow what Dad has done with me. I'd take good care of the kid, bring him places, hug and kiss him a lot, and let him know how proud he makes me. While I'm sure that for most people it's real hard bringing up a kid alone, watching Dad makes it seem only medium difficult.

*"I'm thankful to be part
of such a stable family."*

Ramon,
age 13

When I was born, my mother was twenty years old
and living with my father, but they weren't married. A
few months later she told him to leave, because he was
on drugs. From then on she raised me by herself.

Although I don't remember this, Mom says we were
very poor after that and had to go on welfare. Not until
I was two and Mom started working full-time at a deli
did things get better. Pretty soon we were able to get
off welfare and were never on it again.

While Mom worked during the day I went to nursery
school. At seven-thirty in the morning she would drop
me off there, and she would pick me up at six in the
evening. Sometimes I missed her, but mostly I was happy

at school, because two of Mom's friends were the teachers and they treated me special.

On the days Mom had to work late, one of these teachers would call a taxi driver she knew, and he would take me to Mom's store. The minute I got there, I'd sit down behind the counter and Mom would give me a sandwich and chips to eat. Lots of the people who came in and out of the store knew me, so I got plenty of attention.

After I finished kindergarten at the nursery, Mom enrolled me in a private, Catholic school, where I stayed until the end of sixth grade. When classes were over around three o'clock, I'd go to my great-grandmother's house, which was nearby. Besides watching me, she baby-sat other kids, so I always had friends to play with.

During my last year at Catholic school, when I was eleven, Mom gave me my own key, and from then on I've let myself into an empty house. That has never been a problem for me. Because I paint and draw, I like the quiet and I can concentrate better.

Meanwhile, all this time Mom worked real hard, and although I didn't realize it then, she now tells me that we still had very little money. Yet I never felt poor. She kept the apartment nice and didn't complain about not having enough—at least not in front of me—so I had no idea what the situation was like. Whenever I'd ask her for a He-Man figure I had seen on TV, she'd say she couldn't buy it at that exact moment, but when she got her paycheck on Friday maybe then we could go to the store and pick one out. I still remember when Mom bought me Moss-Man, my favorite figure, and the castle that went with the set.

Throughout these years my father only came to see me once, when I was very young. That day he took me to visit his mother (my other grandma). I haven't seen or spoken to her since then. Now I only meet my father by accident on the street.

The last time we met was six weeks ago, when I was visiting my old neighborhood. He told me he was in a drug rehabilitation program and said maybe soon the two of us could start doing things together. Before we said good-bye, he gave me his telephone number, but I haven't called him yet. I'm afraid that when I do, I might tell him how hard it's been since he left, and maybe he'll get mad. Then he might not want to see me again, and I'll lose him completely. I love my dad. He's my father! Whenever we meet, he hugs and kisses me and asks how I'm doing in school.

While none of my friends has a dad at home, it doesn't make me feel any better—I still miss my father. When I was younger, Mom tried to take his role by playing kickball in the park with me along with my friends and their mothers. That was okay then, but as I got older, I needed a dad to teach me more complicated sports. Since he wasn't around, I had to learn on my own by either watching how the big kids threw the ball or by asking them to show me what to do. In time I got to be a pretty good athlete, and today I'm on the baseball All-Stars. What hurts is that my father is never there to watch me play, even though, more than once, he's promised to come.

At least I can count on Mom's word when she says she's going to be at my game. And sometimes that means she has to rush home from work. Even on Saturday mornings, her one day to sleep late, she's up early to bring me to the field.

All through the years Mom has tried hard to do everything to make me happy. If I was in a school play, she and my aunt would come to see me and they would be so proud. Later on, while she'd brag and brag, I'd tell her how much it hurt that my dad hadn't shown up. She'd hold me and we'd talk about this, and Mom would say that she knew how I felt. When I cried, she'd cry, too. She'd say it wasn't easy for her either and that she was doing her best. Only now am I beginning to understand what she meant.

Going way back, Mom did everything to make me feel I was part of a real family. Even though she worked all day, she'd come home at night full of energy. Together, we'd cook dinner, and after we had eaten, she'd get on the floor with me and we'd play with my toys.

From the time I was young, I had to help her around the house. Early on she gave me chores, which in some ways made me feel that I was an adult. Whenever I carried heavy packages home from the supermarket or rearranged the living room furniture with her, she'd compliment me for doing a man's job. I never felt any of this was too much for me. If my friends asked what I was doing on a certain day, I'd say, "Painting the kitchen," which to me seemed like the most grown-up job in the world.

The year I was seven, Mom and my cousin Mikey's father made an enormous joint birthday party for us two kids. They rented a huge hall and had music and a piñata filled with candy. I thought a hundred people were there, but Mom says it was more like thirty. Whatever, she made me feel very important.

And so did the rest of the family. Every week we'd visit Aunt Linda and Uncle Paul, and they treated me special. Aunt Linda is Mom's sister and is graduating college. Some nights I stay over at her house and have fun with my uncle and play with my cousin David, who's now three years old. Since I've been around David so much, he considers me his older brother.

Yet, with all this, I've always felt there was something missing in my life. When Mom took me to an amusement park and wouldn't go on the roller coaster with me, I'd think, A dad wouldn't refuse if he were here. It got to the point where it didn't even have to be my own father. I just wanted an adult male to hang around with, who would protect me in case robbers broke into the house at night.

Finally, two years ago, after being on the list for so long, I got assigned a Big Brother, named Larry. He likes sports, and until recently, when he got rid of his car, he'd come here every week and we'd play catch or he'd teach me how to play tennis. We've gone to see the Yankees together, and when the Super Bowl was on TV, we went to his friend's house to watch the game. When I'm with Larry, my mind's off Dad for a while.

Even though I keep out of trouble, Mom's not a hundred percent relaxed. That's why she's so strict with me, I think. When I come in from school at three-fifteen, she calls to make sure I'm okay and that I'm getting ready to do my homework. Later, when she gets home in the evening, she checks my work to see that it's done. No other eight graders I hang around with have mothers who keep such an eye on them. While all my friends are outside playing ball I'm indoors doing assignments, and that makes me mad.

Still, I sometimes understand why Mom's so frightened. Five years ago, when we finally got a car, the radio was stolen and then the tires were slashed—in our neighborhood, which was supposed to be safe.

And because of my father's drug problem, Mom is afraid that the same thing could happen to me. Again and again she reminds me of how drugs have ruined his life. Mom may be terrified that I might follow in Dad's footsteps, but drugs are not what I want to do. I'm more interested in becoming a professional ballplayer and an artist on the side.

As I think about it, I'm a lucky kid. I'm thankful to

be part of such a stable family. Other than my father, nobody else has gotten involved in drugs. Because of all the attention I have gotten from Mom and my other relatives, I know I'll be okay when I grow up.

Ramon

"Since my parents have been living apart, I've become closer to each of them individually."

Erin, age 9

The year I was in first grade, my parents got divorced. Although I had known something was wrong, since they kept having loud fights, I didn't understand what divorce was about. I thought it meant that once Dad was gone, I would never see him again.

Even after I started sleeping over at his house, I was still upset, because I was used to spending time with both of my parents together. I was afraid that Dad might take my younger sister, Kim, and me far away and force us to stay with him. It was a very confusing time. Even Mom didn't know how to make me feel better. I was very angry. Pretty soon I was raising my voice to her and Dad too, and I had lots of fights with Kim.

To make things worse, my friend Phoebe's parents had gotten divorced about a year before, and she hardly saw her father. Then, when her mother sent her to boarding school, she was barely with either of her parents. More than anything this really scared me. I thought the same thing might happen to me.

Aside from Phoebe, my friend Sabrina lived with just her mom too, although I'm not sure why, and so did some other kids in my school. At least I didn't feel so different there, and nobody ever made fun of me. Yet it really hurt when I visited friends who had two parents at home and heard them talk about the special things they did as a family. It reminded me that Kim and I would no longer be going on vacations with Mom and Dad together or out for dinner as a family of four.

Although Mom still took Kim and me skiing, it was hard just having one parent around. Whenever we went on the chair lift, she'd sit with my sister, who's the youngest, while I had to go up by myself or with a stranger.

In school too, I had problems because of living with just one parent. When my second grade teacher told us to interview our mother and father and other close relatives for a family tree, I couldn't get all the information. Around then I wasn't seeing Dad that much, and my grandparents and aunts and uncles on his side of the family weren't talking to Mom. When I had to tell my teacher that I felt uncomfortable calling any of them, I was so embarrassed. I was sure she'd think Dad and the rest of the family no longer cared about me.

All these sudden changes made me very unhappy. Not only did Dad's side of the family seem to disappear from our life, Mom wasn't around as much. Once she became a single parent, she started working at two jobs and went to college at night to finish up her degree.

Now that she's done with school, at least I sometimes have her to myself, when Kim stays overnight at a friend's house. Usually then Mom will practice soccer or baseball with me or we'll go out for dinner. But when Kim's at home, we have to share our mother. If Mom brings the two of us to the tennis courts, my sister and I argue over who will play with her first.

Yet since my parents have been living apart, I've become closer to each of them individually. Probably if Dad were still here, I'd run to Mom with my problems and wouldn't confide in him. Then I wouldn't have found out that Dad is such a good listener and an understanding person, too.

The other day I told him that I wasn't happy with the calls the umpire on my baseball team was making, and he talked to me about it, so that soon I felt better. He's also very protective. When I'm with him, I feel safe. But as I said before, that's not how it always was.

Two years ago Kim and I started going to a therapist, because we were worried that our parents were still not getting along and we were sure it was our fault. Sometimes the therapist called in the whole family, and I'd tell Mom and Dad how their fighting was hurting me. The four of us didn't meet that often, but when we did, it really helped. The most important thing I learned was that Mom and Dad still loved me even if I was angry with them.

Today Kim and I see much more of Dad than when he and Mom first divorced. We're at his house two nights a week and alternate weekends. The rest of the time we're with Mom. At her house, we have to do our homework as soon as we come in from school, and then later she'll help us with any problem we have. Dad, though, doesn't care what time our homework gets done as long as it's finished before the night's over. Except for this one thing, the rules are pretty much the same, so I don't feel too mixed up.

Now that my parents aren't living together, they co-operate more. If Dad finds out at the last minute that he has to work on the day he was supposed to have us, he'll call Mom and ask her to keep us, and she usually says okay. Mom is pretty easygoing and tells Dad not to worry when he has to change his plans. She says it's no trouble having us stay with her. But I don't like when Dad cancels dates, no matter what the reason. It doesn't happen often, but when it does, I think visitations are a real pain.

Still, if it were up to me, I'd have my family situation remain the way it is today. Now that I'm old enough to understand that my parents won't get married to each other again, I'd rather they remained unmarried for-ever. Otherwise, it will be confusing to have more than one mother and father. Although both of them date, so far neither has been very serious with another person, and I'm glad about that. Both of them told Kim and me that if they found someone they'd like to marry, they'd talk to us beforehand so we could tell them our feelings. I hope it never gets to that point. With two parents who care so much about me, I wouldn't want anyone else in the picture.

Top to bottom, Erin, Kim

*"I'm happy to have a
nice mother and father."*

Kim,
age 8

My sister, Erin, and I are just a year apart. When I
was in kindergarten and she was in first grade, our parents got divorced. Mom tried to explain what was happening, but I didn't understand what she was talking
about. I was sure my father would be coming home
again.

Then one time when we were supposed to spend the
day with him, he took Erin and me to California without
telling Mom where we were going. She didn't know
where we were or when we'd get back. It was so scary.
I thought I'd never see Mom again.

Finally Dad brought us home, and after that, we all
had to go to court so the judge could decide on the

custody arrangements. That's when I realized my parents' marriage was over.

Since then Erin and I have lived most days with Mom, but we see our father a lot because he lives nearby. At his house, we have our own room and have made friends with two girls in his building who go to our school. One of them lives full-time with her father, while her mother has an apartment in the city. Also, there's a boy in my class who lives with one parent too, because his mother died. So I'm not the only kid with a single parent.

As soon as it was just Mom at home, she started hiring baby-sitters to take care of Erin and me. I hated when she wasn't there to tuck me in bed and give me a good-night kiss. Once she was playing tennis and didn't come home when she usually did. I got so frightened and started crying. The baby-sitter kept telling me not to worry, but that didn't make me feel better. She would say the same thing if I had a stomachache. Mom and Dad, though, would take me seriously if I felt sick or if something worried me. That's why I like it more when one of them is in the house.

Although most of the kids I'm friends with have two parents at home, I don't notice them doing things that differently from my family. Mom bikes with us to town to get ice cream, just like anyone else's mother. And she takes us on vacations. Now that Dad's not with us, she sometimes invites another single mother to come too, which is okay if I like the kids they bring along.

Since our parents got divorced, Erin and I spend more

time with each of them separately. Last summer Dad took us fishing, something Mom doesn't like to do. And Mom plays tennis with us, a game Dad doesn't enjoy. We also go on more vacations—one with Dad and another with Mom. If our parents were still married, this would never happen.

Luckily, Dad lives close by, so I see him much more than other kids I know whose parents are divorced. He even comes on my class trips. And on weekends he watches my sister when she has a soccer game. The only problem is that at the games, he and Mom don't stand next to each other like the other parents. If I'm with Mom and I want to talk to Dad, I have to go over to him, which can be embarrassing. The kids I know who are around must wonder what's going on. Since Mom and Dad no longer act mad, I don't understand why they won't stay near each other in public.

While I've told the friends I can trust about my family situation, I don't want the word spread, even though it's not that bad having Mom as a single parent.

The best part about living with her is that she takes me clothes shopping and has good taste. In that department, Dad would probably do better with a son. He never picks out what I like, or he gets me the wrong size and has to return it.

Still, I have a good time with him, especially when we go off alone and Erin's with Mom. The only trouble is that he doesn't always bring me home on time, and then Mom and Erin worry. Since the time he took us to California, we're all afraid it might happen again. In two parent families, a father would tell the mother he was taking the kids to the movies and would say the exact time they'd be back and keep his word. But when parents are divorced, they don't talk about the plans as much, and then it causes everybody to get upset. If it wasn't for this, being with a single parent would be pretty much the same as being with a mom and dad.

But if I can, I still will avoid raising children on my own. I want my kids to grow up with a mother and a father in the same house. My one wish in the world, which probably won't come true, is to have my parents solve things immediately and come back to each other. Since it's not going to happen, I'm happy to have a nice mother and father.

Guidelines for Living with a Single Parent

After reading many books and articles about single parent families, speaking to therapists who work with these families, and completing the interviews for *Living with a Single Parent*, I feel that certain basic strategies will help children fare better in this type of family situation. The most important ones are listed below.

1.   It takes time to adjust to living with a single parent, especially if it's happened unexpectedly. Naturally, you're going to feel loss. You've lost a live-in parent and the way your family used to be, and there may be sudden changes. For example, the amount of money your family has to live on probably will become more limited. Other

changes may affect how available your parent is and the number of chores you're expected to do. Go easy on yourself, and talk to your parent about what all this means for you instead of keeping your worries inside.

2. Try to be aware of your feelings. Don't put on a happy face when you are feeling miserable. Although your parent may be having his or her own difficulties, you're not helping yourself by pretending everything is okay. The sooner sad feelings come out in the open, the faster they can begin to heal.

3. Mostly all children living with a single parent secretly wish their mother and father would get back together again. In most cases, this is just a fantasy, and if it's held on to for too long, it makes it harder to get on with your life. While living with a single parent might not be your choice, you'll feel more relieved if you accept the situation and concentrate on creating better relationships with each of your parents separately.

4. If you're living with a parent of the opposite sex, sleep in a separate bed from that parent and, if possible, in a separate room. Try to find an adult of your sex to confide in about things you feel too uncomfortable about sharing with the parent who's at home.

5. If you're caught in a family situation you don't like—

perhaps being made your parent's confidant or being used as a go-between by your mother and father— muster up the courage to tell your parent or parents how you feel and that you don't want to be put in this role.

6. In some single parent families, children are physically or sexually abused by their parent. Maybe the adult is an alcoholic or on drugs. If any of this describes what goes on in your family, you need to get professional help immediately. Go right to your school therapist if one is available, or tell your school nurse. Either can offer help and advise where you or your family can get counseling. Calling your doctor or clergyman is another good idea, as is seeking out the special groups that are listed at the end of this book.

7. When you're feeling low and confused in general, talk to someone you feel close to, preferably an adult. If you have a good relationship with one or both of your parents, by all means go to them first. Otherwise, ask your teacher if there's a school program where kids living with single parents can get together and share their concerns. It's comforting to know there are others experiencing similar problems.

8. The single parent usually has a busy schedule, trying to work and run the house smoothly. It may happen that there is less time for you than there had been in

the past, especially if your parent is dating. If you feel left out, tell your parent and ask him or her to set aside special time just for the two of you.

9. It makes no sense to manipulate your parents to get your way. Telling one parent that you favor the other because he or she is more generous or more lenient will only cause further irritation between the two of you, and it may make your parents less tolerant of each other. Instead, have sensible talks about why some rules bother you, and then work together on changing them.

10. It is extremely important to have your own interests. The more you're good at, the more confidence you'll have in yourself. Also, make time to be with friends you enjoy. It's healthy to have fun. Take care of yourself. Keep working hard in school and pay attention to how you look. When you see yourself in the mirror and can smile, you'll feel a lot happier.

11. There are positive aspects of living with a single parent, and these should not be ignored. For instance, you may no longer have to listen to the fighting that once went on in your house. And there's only one parent now to make the rules, so that's less confusing. Also, you may now be able to develop closer one-to-one relationships with each of your parents. Try to remember that there are many different kinds of families today

and yours is not as unusual as you may believe. Living with a single parent may not be what you hoped for, but your family is still a unit. If you all work together, you'll feel part of a team.

Bibliography

FOR CHILDREN

Dolmetsch, Paul, and Alexa Shik. *The Kids' Book about Single-Parent Families.* New York: Doubleday, 1985.

An informative book offering advice on how to make the single parent living arrangement an easier one. Ages: 10–14.

Gardner, Richard. *The Boys' and Girls' Book about One-Parent Families.* New York: G. P. Putnam's Sons, 1978.

A good vehicle to open discussion between parents and children living in a single parent household. Cartoon illustrations lighten the content of the text. Ages: 6–11.

Gilbert, Sara. *How to Live with a Single Parent.* New York: Lothrop, Lee & Shepard, 1982.

A how-to book for preteens and teenagers living with a single parent. Discusses issues that might arise and how to resolve them, sometimes by getting outside help. Ages: 9 and older.

Krementz, Jill. *How It Feels When a Parent Dies.* New York: Alfred A. Knopf, 1981.

Eighteen children express their feelings about the death of their parent and what life has been like for them since. Ages: 9 and older.

————*How It Feels When Parents Divorce.* New York: Alfred A. Knopf, 1984.

Children ages seven through sixteen tell what it's like for them now that their parents are divorced. Ages: 9 and older.

Le Shan, Eda. *Learning to Say Good-By: When a Parent Dies.* New York: Macmillan, 1976.

A comforting book for children who have lost a parent through death. Talks about the children's feelings and those of the adults close to them. Ages: 8–12.

Rofes, Eric. *The Kids' Book about Death and Dying—By and for Kids.* Boston: Little, Brown, 1985.

Explores the subject of death, whether it be of a parent, friend, or pet, from questions asked by children at the Fayerweather Street School in Massachusetts. Ages: 11–14.

Rosenberg, Maxine B. *Being Adopted*. New York: Lothrop, Lee & Shepard, 1984.

Profiles the feelings and experiences of three transracially adopted children—one the author's child—describing the unique circumstances of families formed in this way. Photographs. Ages: 6–10.

————*Growing Up Adopted*. New York: Bradbury Press, 1989.

Interviews with fourteen adoptees—eight children and six adults—by author, who is an adoptive parent. Each reveals feelings about what adoption has meant over a period of time. Transracial adoptees, disabled adoptees, and those adopted at an older age included. Ages: 9 and older.

FOR ADULTS

Atlas, Stephen L. *Single Parenting*. Englewood Cliffs, N.J.: Prentice-Hall, 1981.

From a man's point of view, how to create a wholesome, viable single parent household where all members of the family can grow.

Dodson, Fitzhugh. *How to Single Parent*. New York: Harper & Row, 1987.

How to cope as a single parent—dealing with your feelings and how to help your children.

Garfinkel, Irwin, and Sara S. McLanahan. *Single Mothers and their Children*. Washington, D.C.: Urban Institute Press, 1986.

Findings of single parent homes. Effects on the children and the single mother.

Greywolf, Elizabeth S. *The Single Mother's Handbook.* New York: William Morrow, 1984.

The difficulties and rewards of being a single mom. Based on interviews with hundreds of women in this situation.

Pearson, Carol Lynn. *One on the Seesaw.* New York: Random House, 1988.

A personal story of a divorced woman raising two boys and two girls on her own. Warm, witty, and moving.

Wallenstein, Judith S., and Sandra Blakeslee. *Second Chances.* New York: Ticknor & Fields, 1989.

Findings of 130 people affected by divorce. Examines the repercussions five and then ten years after the experience.

Sources of Help

Al-Anon/Alateen Family Group Headquarters
P.O. Box 862
Midtown Station
New York, N.Y. 10018
1-800-344-2666 (Including Alaska, Hawaii, Puerto Rico, and
Virgin Islands)
1-212-302-7240 (New York and Canada)

24-hour answering service

Association for Children with Learning Disabilities
4156 Library Road
Pittsburgh, Pa. 15234
1-412-341-1515

Referral organization for children and adults with learning
difficulties. Individual chapters throughout the United
States.

Big Brothers/Big Sisters of America
117 S. 17th Street, Suite 1200
Philadelphia, Pa. 19103

Matches adults with single parent kids. See local telephone
book for area listing.

Childhelp USA
Child Abuse Hotline USA-National
1-800-4-A-CHILD (1-800-422-4453)

Family Anonymous
1-800-736-9805

For families of drug addicts—to learn how to take care of
themselves. See listing in area telephone directory.

Family Service Association of America (FSAA)
44 East 23rd Street
New York, N.Y. 10010
1-212-674-6100

Offers counseling and support for families and individuals.

International Youth Council of Parents Without Partners
8807 Colesville Road
Silver Spring, Md. 20910
1-301-588-9354

Teenage division of Parents Without Partners. Offers support
and social activities.

National Council on Alcoholism
12 West 21st Street
New York, N.Y. 10010
1-800-NCA-CALL (1-800-622-2255)

The National Council on Family Relations
3989 Central Avenue N.E.
Columbia Heights, Minn. 55421
1-612-781-9331

Computerized file of single parent groups across the country.

National Institute on Drug Abuse Hotline
1-800-843-4971

Information provided for alcohol and drug problems.

National Runaway Switchboard
1-800-621-4000

Offers help to runaways and assists them if they want to contact relatives.

National Youth Crisis Hotline
1-800-662-HELP (1-800-662-4357)

For intervention when there's a crisis at home.

North American Council on Adoptable Children
1821 University Avenue, Suite 275
St. Paul, Minn. 55104
1-612-644-3036

Lists current publications about adoption and offers re-
sources and technical assistance for those involved with adoption.

Parents Without Partners, Inc.
International Headquarters
8807 Colesville Road
Silver Spring, Md. 20910
1-301-588-9354

Largest single parent organization in America. Advocates for
single parents and children. Publishes *The Single Parent* jour-
nal. See telephone book for local chapters.

Single Mothers by Choice
P.O. Box 1642
Gracie Square Station
New York, N.Y. 10028
1-212-988-0993

National organization with chapters in every state and Canada. Provides support and information for women who
choose to be single parents. Newsletter.

Single Parent Resource Center
141 West 28th Street
New York, N.Y. 10001
1-212-949-0221

Telephone information and referral service on any subject
of concern to single parents.

THEOS
11609 Frankstown Road
Pittsburgh, Pa. 15235

Nonreligious support group for widowed adults. Works with
other social service organizations.

Index